Doors To Transformation
My Mother – My Self

© 2014 Nicole Lawrence

All Rights Reserved. The author grants no assignable permission to reproduce for resale or redistribution. This license is limited to the individual purchaser and does not extend to others. Permission to reproduce these materials for any other purpose must be obtained in writing from the publisher except for the use of brief quotations within book chapters.

Disclaimer

All rights reserved. No part of this book may be used or reproduced by any means, graphic, scanning, electronic, or mechanical, including photocopying, recording, taping or by any information storage retrieval system without the written permission of the publisher except in the case of brief quotations embodied in critical articles and reviews.

For more information or to contact Nicole, go to http://nicolelawrence.com.

Because of the dynamic nature of the Internet, any web addresses or links contained in this book may have changed since publication and may no longer be valid. The views expressed in this work are solely those of the author and do not necessarily reflect the views of the publisher, and the publisher hereby disclaims any responsibility for them.

The author of this book does not dispense medical advice or prescribe the use of any technique as a form of treatment for physical, emotional, or medical problems without the advice of a physician, either directly or indirectly. The intent of the author is only to offer information of a general nature to help you in your quest for emotional and spiritual wellbeing.

In the event you use any of the information in this book for yourself, which is your constitutional right, the author and the publisher assume no responsibility for your actions.

Published by M&B Global Solutions Inc.
United States of America (USA)
ISBN: 978-1-942731-10-8

Doors To Transformation

My Mother – My Self

Nicole Lawrence

Dedication

For all mothers and daughters

Table of Contents

Preface 9

Chapter 1 - The Call 13

Chapter 2 - A Look Back 19

Chapter 3 - My Journey Begins 25

Chapter 4 - Beginning the Healing 31

Chapter 5 - The Layers of Process 45

Chapter 6 - Encountering Shame 67

Chapter 7 - Beliefs and Patterns 73

Chapter 8 - Preverbal and Prenatal 81

Chapter 9 - Our Inner Child 87

Chapter 10 - Changing the Milestones 93

Chapter 11 - The Seeds of Understanding 97

Chapter 12 – Forgiveness 105

Chapter 13 - Gifts from Difficulties 109

Chapter 14 - Closing the Circle 115

A Note for Those Adopted 125

Acknowledgements 126

Resources 128

About the Author 130

Preface

We all have a mother, the greatest of us and the least of us. Whether physical, adoptive or stepmother, good, bad or indifferent, we've been influenced by her presence. The dictionary defines "Mother" as both a noun - a female parent; a woman who has given birth to a child, and a verb - to give birth to; to watch over and protect in a motherly way. We learned about love, caring and nurturing from our mother. Usually, they are our first bonding experience. Our relationship with our mother sets the foundation for our relationship with ourselves.

For some of us, however, the love and caring were interspersed or overrun by abuse, abandonment and/or neglect. If our mothers were unable to be there for us, or were there in abusive ways, then we have conditioning, hurts and pains to come to terms with, to heal, and make peace with if we choose.

If this is the case, then it falls to us to re-mother ourselves. In the Greek Myths, Gaia, the Earth Mother, created herself out of primordial chaos. The symbology is that we can rebirth ourselves out of the chaos of our negative childhoods. Giving birth to ourselves anew is part of the transformation process.

In re-mothering ourselves, we need to look to those qualities most associated with mothering: love, nurturing, caring, patience, humor, and strength - all qualities we need to use with ourselves in our process of transformation and re-mothering.

This book is my story of coming to peace with my mother. It is part of the journey of my life, and in writing about it, I realized it is a journey all of us go through in one way or another.

This book is a tool for exploring and doing healing work with issues around your mother and yourself. It is a starting point and in no way is meant to be deep therapy. It's a place to begin to look at what you might want to change in yourself. It is by no means the be all and end all - it is not even a "How-To" book. It is more of a "You can do it, too," book meant to inspire and cheer you on. I share a couple of techniques, but mostly I reference what worked for me and share where to find more information that may be of help on your journey.

Perhaps you are familiar with emotional release work. When we don't express and release emotions in a healthy way, they can remain stored within us causing stress, and some people believe, even illness. Releasing and expressing emotions isn't about throwing things around or being abusive to yourself or others. It does mean being willing to feel your feelings completely until they are done. If you have concerns about this or feel your emotions may be too much, see a certified counselor or therapist in your area.

In healing our relationships with our mothers, we heal our relationship with ourselves and, I firmly believe, we assist in healing those relationships for the world at large. We are attending and mending our corner of the fabric of life, of which we are a part.

My thank you gift to you for purchasing this book can be found at http://nicolelawrence.com/doors-to-transformation-gift/

Chapter 1
The Call

My mother took her green eyes with her when she died.

"You'd better come, she's not doing well," Michael, my stepfather, said over the phone.

When I flew to Palm Springs (Calif.) this time, I didn't know it would be for my mother's death. Three months before, my mother found out she had lung cancer. The doctors had given her one round of chemo and said that with more she might be able to last two years; without, six months. Her body had a horrible reaction to the first round, and it didn't look like any more was possible. To add to this, they hadn't told her it was terminal.

My sister, Deb, and I had been to see her a few times since the diagnosis. My stepfather would call, telling us she was getting bad again, and I'd fly out from my home in Hawaii. My sister, living in the Northwest, flew down from there to Palm Springs. Sometimes I visited Mom alone and other times my sister visited her alone. Invariably, Mom would rally when we got there. She'd be in bed looking pale and frail, and then announce that she wanted to go out to eat at her favorite restaurant. Out we'd go, and she was perky and full of life.

So when I got another call from my stepfather telling me, "She isn't doing well, you should come," I wondered if it would be the same as the other times. I questioned myself, did I really need to go? Could my sister, Debbie, go this time?

Right then I turned it over to the Universe and said, "If I'm supposed to see Mom, show me. Let me have a sign."

I called the airlines to see about availability - often the flights into and out of the smaller Hawaiian Islands can be booked. I was thinking maybe I'd get a flight the next evening or a couple of days at the most. When the reservation agent came on the line, I told her I needed to go see my mom who was sick. She put me on hold for a moment, came back and said, "I've got you on a flight that leaves in four hours." OK, Universe, I guess that is my sign. I hurriedly threw things in a suitcase and ran out the door hoping to even make the flight.

Mom had emphysema for a couple of years before the cancer. The doctors had said she'd likely have six months to two years with chemo. Unfortunately, she had a bad reaction to the first round of chemo and ended up with a severe infection. The doctors didn't think she could handle any more. I suggested to my stepdad that he call Hospice - I had heard they were really good at helping families with the dying process.

"Oh, no. We couldn't have them here – your mother is too afraid," Michael told me over the phone. He went on to tell me about how her doctor went to take out the stint for administering chemo and she freaked out. My mother couldn't go near the thought of dying. She'd panic at the thought. So my stepdad and the doctor let her think that she was going to get better, and they were going to do another round of chemotherapy when she was strong enough. So even mentioning Hospice around her was taboo.

If it was me, I'd have wanted to know I was dying. I harbored some reservations about the way my stepdad was handling my mom's fears. I wondered if it was partly to protect himself from Mom's reactions. On the other hand, I also understood his concerns; my mom could be wildly unreasonable and pitch major fits.

In the end, I let it be. Mom's doctor had agreed with my stepdad about not telling her. In addition, she would have had to have learned weeks before to come to terms within herself, and she didn't have that time now. I also believed that some greater part of her knew what was going on and decided to trust that.

I made the flight from Hawaii and got to Palm Springs in the early hours of the morning, rented a car and drove straight to the house. Mom was glad to see me. Seeing her in her bed at home, I could tell she was more frail than before. The cancer had taken its toll, but she still had a sparkle to her personality.

We spent some time talking and catching up. This time of transition with my mom showed me how much I'd grown in myself, though I didn't see it at the time. It was only later in looking back that I was able to see it.

* * *

Petite and vivacious with flashing Kelly-green eyes, my mother loved being the life of the party – any party. Her friends referred to her as "Queen Bee." My Aunt Helen, my mother's younger sister, once told me that my mother was popular and a natural athlete in school. "All of the teams and clubs wanted her; the swim club, the diving club and the drama club. She was like a golden girl, she was good at everything."

My mom adopted green as her signature color. She often wore green to match her eyes and chose to write only in green ink. She'd buy boxes of viridian Flair™ felt-tip pens and keep them in her desk drawer. She wore green jewelry. She especially loved jade pendants, earrings and rings.

My mother was also an alcoholic. She and my father separated and then divorced when I was five. Although I had siblings, I grew up alone with her. It was challenging and confusing to grow up with a parent who drank. She began in the evenings after 5:00 or so and was drunk most nights. I can remember only one time she wasn't so drunk – a night we sat in the living room and read to each other. Most nights she watched television with an Old Grand-Dad bourbon in hand.

Despite her drinking, my mother was generous to a fault. She didn't engage in deep conversations, but would mostly listen. At parties she'd nod and say, "Oh, I agree," when asked her opinion. Even when people weren't addressing her, sometimes in her inebriation she mistakenly thought they were. I have more than one memory of being out to dinner with my mother and her friends, and people at the next table were having their picture taken. Mom thought they were taking her picture, to which she loudly objected.

What my mom latched onto were situations where someone voiced a desire for something they didn't have a way of getting. She'd start planning how to give it to them, a way to make it a surprise. She often gave them what they wanted and more. Sometimes it was something for a stranger she'd heard of on the late night news. My mom loved to be the giver, the bearer of gifts. It endeared people to her and often attracted those who wanted to use her – a pattern I've had to learn to heal in myself as well.

I don't know that any one thing started her drinking. I suspect it was many things that built up; issues and pain she never dealt with plus the cocktail, highball, and drinking tradition of the 1950s that granted a sort of permission to drown your sorrows. I see now that she had her own losses and dashed dreams, crushed hopes and disappointments, and used the drinking as a way to numb out.

While my mother was numbing out, I was developing beliefs and patterns around abuse and neglect that took me years of inner work in my adult years to heal.

Chapter 2

A Look Back

Initially, after the divorce and before we were separated, my brother Larry, my sister Deb and I traveled back and forth between Dad and Mom. We saw Dad some days of the week and Mom on the other days.

In my memory, my sister did most of my and Larry's care-taking when we were at Mom's. Debbie is the one I remember getting me dressed in the mornings and reading me bedtime stories at night. I always wanted a horse story, usually "Misty of Chincoteague." My sister taught me to tell time, "Where is the big hand and where is the little hand?"

It was my sister I ran to the first time I got the white laces on my little red Keds™ sneakers to tie into a bow. Patiently, over and over she showed me how to, "Hold the loop with one finger, and wrap the other lace around and pull it through." Off by myself, I would mimic what she had done, only to wander around with trailing laces and have her tie them up again. She was the one who played with my brother and me.

Debbie took Larry and me hand in hand on Sundays to the church down the street. Afterward, she read to me from the Sunday comics while Larry lifted pictures with a wad of Silly Putty. Sometimes I was allowed tea with sugar as a treat.

Newly divorced, Mom partied and had people at the house at all hours. I have a collage of memories of that time - men I didn't know asleep on the sofas in the morning; Larry in pajamas drinking what was left in the glasses sitting out from the party the night before; us shuttling back and forth to Dad's and my stepmother - who always seemed to disapprove of us. My only constants in the chaos were my brother and sister.

* * *

At times my sister, brother and I would compare notes from our childhood. Often, events we shared by experience, we saw from different perspectives and had come to different understandings.

Specific events rise like outcroppings out of the swirling currents of memory. Some are smooth and some cut with jagged edges. Others journeying with you down the same tributary are given only a glancing blow by the one that hit you full force – the one that knocked the wind out of you, forcing a turn in the direction of your life.

It was hard for me each time Mom drove us back to Dad's and I'd start crying. One day, Dad had had enough. The way I remember it, he got mad and I found myself having to choose between him and Mom. Literally I was between them physically, Dad on one side and Mom on the other. Dad wanted me to live with him and I remember Mom saying, "She wants to be with her Mother." At five, I still wanted to be with my mother.

I thought all of us were going to live with Mom and I ran to tell Debbie. She said, "We're living with Dad." Then I was alone in the car with Mom driving away. It seemed like a long time before I saw Debbie and Larry again.

* * *

I couldn't have known at that age the trauma it would be to be alone with my mother, and I was never offered an option to return to live with my father. I suspect my mother took pills as well as drank too much. At night she regularly hallucinated about people who weren't there and events that hadn't happened. This went on even into my teen years.

Often I woke with a start to bumping, thumping, slurred whispers, and the specter of my mother weaving at the foot of my bed. Sometimes she would trail away toward her room in childlike laughter. Other times, I woke to her telling me to be quiet, covering my mouth with fumbling hands. There were times she'd be on the floor in a heap sobbing and mumbling. I often heard her whispering and talking at night to people who weren't there.

Shortly after going to live with my mom, she stumbled into my room crying in the middle of the night.

"Honey wake up."

"Mom?" I said, sitting up.

On that night, Mom insisted that my sister, Debbie, was hiding under her bed. "I can't get her to come out. Go tell her to come out right now!" I remember thinking, "Debbie? I haven't seen her in so long!"

I was still at an age that I believed what adults told me. I didn't understand about alcoholism.

When Mom told me Debbie was hiding under her bed, I believed her. I ran to the room really expecting to see my sister under my mother's bed. Of course there was only empty space. Mom kept asking, "Don't you see her?"

Then she told me someone out on the street was trying to get her and she wanted me to save her. I looked out the window in the night and only saw an empty street and a lone streetlamp. Then she was talking to someone who wasn't there. I became more and more afraid. I did not know who she was when she was like this and it terrified me. Nothing was as it should be with my mother.

Not every night was as bad as this, but there were many. Sometimes she'd accuse me of something I didn't do – she'd have misplaced something and wanted to know where I'd hidden it. I began to pretend I was asleep whenever I woke and heard her in my room or in the hall. She'd call my name and I wouldn't answer, hoping she'd leave me alone. I didn't have Debbie or Larry to go to or to help me.

When I chose to be with my mom, I was too young to grasp that when you choose for something, you simultaneously make choices away from other things. I rarely saw Debbie and Larry, and when I did, we weren't as close as we'd once been. They seemed more like strangers to me. It was not the three of us anymore. It was the two of them; and me alone with my troubled mother.

I didn't realize what a challenge this was until I began to heal. After I left home, I started the journey that's brought me to my healing.

Chapter 3

My Journey Begins

I think surviving my childhood was due in part to Guardian Angels. That may sound funny, but I think a lot of times what I survived with my mother had a lot to do with Angels looking out for me. A spiritual connection has always been part of my life. I believe you need to lean on the spiritual connection in order to heal and get to a place of forgiveness.

My mother wasn't mean; she wasn't out to hurt me. I came to see, with all of the healing that I went through, that she herself was suffering, and understanding her is part of what gave me the power to forgive. My mother was neglectful, and if it were today's world, I would've been removed from her by some kind of social services. My mother's parents thought my father was looking out for me; my father thought my mother's parents would look out for me; and somehow, I got lost in the middle.

Growing up the way I did, the pain felt normal and I didn't realize it was something I shouldn't have had to experience. The loneliness of being separated from a brother and sister, and the absence of love from my mother who was alcoholic and narcissistic led me to largely accept "just the way life was." It wasn't until junior high and then high school that I began to see that things were not right at home.

In junior high and high school, I had two good friends who each had an alcoholic parent. We grew up with the same patterning, and that made us understand each other. We could also understand each other's parents. We knew how to be around them.

* * *

Spirituality had been a focus for me, and I explored, read books and attended conferences. I didn't realize how much anger and pain I had stored inside me until I was well onto my spiritual path. With all the exploring, I still hadn't understood the impact of my life with my mother. I spent five years with one teacher, and I see now that he and the other students had dysfunctional behaviors.

Around the time I left that group, I came across the book by Melody Beattie, "Codependent No More." When I read that book, things began to fall into place for me. I saw how I had been there for my mother, supporting her in all of her alcoholic behaviors. That book was the first real eye-opener for me to see what alcoholism was, what it does to those around them, and how the behavioral patterns create a network of codependency.

With my next spiritual teacher, Lazaris, I really began the journey of facing, feeling and releasing the years of pain. Lazaris is a channeled entity, and while some people may take exception to that, I received tremendous benefit. For me, the workshops were invaluable for the help they gave me in being able to release the pain and shame that was my conditioning from childhood.

Attending workshops where we looked into our shame, the depths of the pain and the patterning that it produced, I began to see there was a way to heal, a way out. The old traumas began to heal.

Further, I saw that I was not alone – others, too, had had difficult childhoods and were in the process of healing. This was key for me. Growing up I saw that other families were not like mine. My habits and behaviors – which were normal in the situation with my mom – attracted ridicule and humiliation outside of my home. I became so uncomfortable that I began to try and hide.

This need to hide has an opposite effect. It creates a desperate need to belong. Out of this desperate need to belong, I was abandoning who I really was and trying to be what everybody else wanted me to be. Subconsciously, I thought that if I could be what they wanted me to be, I would be accepted.

In the beginning of my process, I had a lot of blame and anger toward my mother. I also encountered feelings of loss. With my mom's neglect and abandonment, I missed out on the mothering I was supposed to have had.

I found I was angry at God and the world. I felt that somehow God had shortchanged me, that the world had shortchanged me. For a long time, I was bitter; but I kept at my process of releasing the emotions and working toward forgiveness. It seemed that as soon as I felt something and released it, another memory would come up. I let the tears flow, I journaled, I meditated, yet I couldn't get to forgiveness – not for a while. As I worked through my hurts, I recognized that it's all part of the process and needed clearing.

As the pain released and dissipated, I began to see things differently. One of the things I saw was that many, many people have grown up in dysfunctional families. There is a whole stratum of society that includes children raised in dysfunctional families who are trying to function in the world. Without doing any healing work, these patterns get passed on because they are accepted as normal.

Part of the healing work includes setting in place new, healthier patterns. Children learn from their parents healthy and unhealthy patterns - depending on how their parents were raised. These patterns get perpetuated. Without working to shift these, they can carry on affecting multiple generations. Negative conditioning doesn't stay within the family; it also plays out in the workplace and society.

There are ways to heal and change these patterns in ourselves, and by doing so, affect those around us and make the world a better place.

Chapter 4
Beginning the Healing

Someone once asked a spiritual leader, "Where do I begin?" His answer was, "Begin where you are, not where you'd like to be."

Begin where you are. It's important to look and see where you are, and determine if you really want to work your way through the healing. It isn't a journey everyone makes. Many people go through their lives without ever looking into their childhood to see about healing. They may not want to. They may be happy with the lives they have.

If you were adopted, you can still do this work. This is about your relationship with whoever was the mother figure in your life -- the one you learned about love from.

I'm not adopted, but I have read and heard that children who were adopted have additional challenges and issues that birth children don't face. There can be feelings of rejection and low self-esteem that create an additional layer of feelings to process. If you are adopted, be gentle with yourself as you work through your process.

Some of the questions may apply beyond the mother that raised you to your birth mother. Try to work through the questions focusing on one parent. Then, if it feels right, go through the questions focusing on your birth mother. You may not be able to answer or have responses to all the questions. You may never have met your birth mother and you may be surprised at what may surface.

In the Resources section of the book, you will find some websites and recommendations for those who are adopted.

* * *

Ask yourself, where are you in your relationship with your mother? This isn't about making your mother see where she was wrong or seeing where you were wrong, or living a life of regret. This is about your inner relationship to your mother, your experiences, your patterns, decisions and beliefs that have gone into creating the life experience you have now.

The memories and issues that are most important will surface. These may not be the earliest memories. They may not be in chronological order. The memories that are most ready to be resolved and released are the ones that surface.

So this is where to begin – with the decision that you want to do this healing work. If you don't have memories that are "up," one of the ways to stir them is to begin by asking yourself questions.

The following question exercise is based on a book I read in the early 1990s. Unfortunately, I'm not able to remember the title or author. It was a wonderful book, chock full of questions on various issues that were designed to help you get a deeper understanding of your issues. I found it a really helpful technique and still develop questions around issues into which I want to go deeper.

These questions are meant to jog your mind and memories. They may stir up feelings and thoughts, and help you see what you would like to heal in relationship to your mother. The answers you uncover are for your own personal understanding and growth. Their value lies in that they reveal your unique inner perspective and provide clues for areas to focus on.

Exercise Directions:

Find a quiet time to do the exercise where you won't be disturbed. After each question are eight blank spaces to fill in. Ask yourself the question and fill in what comes to mind on the first line. Immediately ask yourself the question again, and on the second line fill in the next answer. Repeat the question to yourself, filling in all of the empty lines. Often, the most powerful answers are not the ones at the top of the list, but are further down. If you really draw a blank on the later answers, then put what comes to mind, even if it is a repeat of previous answers.

You don't have to do all the questions in one sitting, but do all the answers for a specific question at one time. All of the empty lines are meant to be filled in during the same sitting.

Doing it this way – allowing the answers to come from within – creates a stream of consciousness. The first few answers may be what you expect, but the later ones may surprise you with deeply revealing answers. They also may be pretty much what you put down at the top of the list.

This isn't about getting the answer right, it's about discovering any deeper perspectives that you may not be aware of. If you find yourself writing nothing but wonderful things and you have a terrible relationship with your mother, you might need to look deeper.

Pdf version of this exercise can be found at

http://nicolelawrence.com/doors-to-transformation-exercises/

When I think about my mother, I feel:

1. _____

2. _____

3. _____

4. _____

5. _____

6. _____

7. _____

8. _____

I wish my mother had been different in this way:

1. _____

2. _____

3. _____

4. _____

5. _____

6. _____

7. _____

8. _____

My mother is:

1. _____

2. _____

3. _____

4. _____

5. _____

6. _____

7. _____

8. _____

What I know about my mother that you would never guess is:

1. _____

2. _____

3. _____

4. _____

5. _____

6. _____

7. _____

8. _____

My mother was only there for me:

1. _____

2. _____

3. _____

4. _____

5. _____

6. _____

7. _____

8. _____

I wish my mother had been more:

1. _____

2. _____

3. _____

4. _____

5. _____

6. _____

7. _____

8. _____

My friend's mother was better because:

1. _____

2. _____

3. _____

4. _____

5. _____

6. _____

7. _____

8. _____

If I had to create the ideal mother, she would be:

1. _____

2. _____

3. _____

4. _____

5. _____

6. _____

7. _____

8. _____

My mother never:

1. _____

2. _____

3. _____

4. _____

5. _____

6. _____

7. _____

8. _____

My mother always:

1. _____

2. _____

3. _____

4. _____

5. _____

6. _____

7. _____

8. _____

What drives me crazy about my mother is:

1. _____

2. _____

3. _____

4. _____

5. _____

6. _____

7. _____

8. _____

What I love about my mother is:

1. _____

2. _____

3. _____

4. _____

5. _____

6. _____

7. _____

8. _____

As I did this work for myself, specific memories came up. I kept a journal and wrote out the events related to any answers that triggered me. Even returning to the questions exercise after a period of a few months or more can reveal deeper and different things.

There are a couple more places in the book where I employ questions as a means to help get clarity. Follow the same procedure as with these questions.

There are levels and layers beyond stirring up memories. Beliefs, patterns and meanings arise out of these events from our past and also need exploring. In the next chapter, we'll begin to delve into these.

Step 5
The Layers of Process

Over time, working through my process, I noticed there were more than just the emotions of what had happened. There was the side of what didn't happen that I wanted to have happen. Beyond both the "event" and "what didn't occur that I'd wished had happened" were layers of assumptions and meanings.

At the time of or just after the painful incident, I drew conclusions of what that meant about me. I also drew conclusions about the others involved and about the world. Out of these meanings and decisions, I formed beliefs that became the filters through which I perceived life.

The process looks like this:

• **The Event That Happened**

• **What Didn't Happen That I Wanted to Happen**

• **What That Means About Me**

   (Both what did and did not happen)

- **What That Means About the Other Person**

    (Both what did and did not happen)

- **What that Means About the World**

    (Both what did and did not happen)

These meanings and decisions became the parameters by which I lived my life. It wasn't conscious – I didn't sit down and think through the meanings – but it did happen. As a child, so much can come at us that we may not be able to process and sort out. We draw conclusions to try and make sense of it.

After this section of describing the segments, there is another series of flow questions you can use to help discover more.

What Happened

It's important to look at and work with the event itself. Review an incident in your mind. Perhaps journal it out – what happened? If there are emotions, spend some time releasing and expressing them in an appropriate way. In my own process, I chose to work with a situation that brought up feelings of anger, rage, humiliation and shame.

Growing up, I was very lucky in that I had a horse for a time. I was horse-crazy and kept begging for one. When I was 10, my mom gave me one. We lived in the suburbs and couldn't have the horse there, so we boarded it at a riding stable. My mom had someone she hired to help out around the house and run errands, and they would take me to the stable after school.

I arrived at the barn one afternoon to find my horse with his mane all braided up like he was going to be in a horse show. I didn't know anything about why he was all done up. The owner of the farm came in and was annoyed, "Where were you?" she asked.

I didn't know what to say or how to answer.

"You were supposed to have been here two hours ago! I told your mother to have you dress in your show clothes and be on time." I could only stand there, stunned.

"The local newspaper is doing an article and they were planning to take a picture of you and your horse. They sent out a photographer." She finished by telling me, "We waited and you never showed up so we put another little girl on your horse and they took the picture."

I was devastated, and angry with my mother. She had forgotten to tell me. She had forgotten all about it. With her drinking she forgot so many things.

Remembering this event at the barn brought up a lot of feelings. At first they were jumbled and a bit vague, but I stayed with the imagery. At times, I slowed it down when I came to a part that had "juice" – more of an emotional charge.

When I felt something specific, I stayed with it, feeling the emotion and letting it move through me.

Some of the first emotions I encountered were rage and frustration. My mother "messed up" again and I felt as if I had lost out. It felt unfair to have to trust my mom when she was so untrustworthy, even with things I was supposed to know but didn't know about. I was embarrassed that I didn't know I was supposed to be in the photograph.

What Didn't Happen That I Wanted to Happen

Releasing the unfelt emotions of the incident was just the first part. It is also important to look at what did not occur that you wished *had* happened. Both sides hold an emotional charge. While the event itself is about the hurts that were, this is about the hurts that weren't.

As I worked with releasing my feeling on what happened at the barn, I saw what did not occur. What I wanted to have happen was for my mom to have remembered – for me to have been dressed and in that picture. Me on my horse. On a deeper level, I wanted my mother to be someone I could trust, who could be there for me. I wanted to know that she cared enough about me to do that.

Often we don't see the hurts that "weren't" until later in life when we reflect back. Seen from an adult perspective, we know what should and should not have happened. We judge ourselves, others or our mother based on these events.

What That Means About Me

Beyond the immediate event are the conclusions you may have drawn about yourself, what you decided it meant to you and about you that it even happened. This includes your reactions/responses or lack of them. We often judge ourselves and draw conclusions on what we did or didn't do in the situation. At the time the events happened, we are often in deep emotions, but underlying are the decisions we make about ourselves. These decisions affect our relationships with our self and others, often for the rest of our lives.

When I found out Mom forgot about my being in the photograph at the barn, I felt humiliated, angry and ashamed. If it had been a single incident, a one-time thing, it probably wouldn't have hit me so hard. It was compounded because my mother forgot things frequently and my horse meant so much to me. I had loved horses for as long as I could remember. This strong connection was part of my identity, and it was these decisions about what it meant that became part of my identity for most of my life.

My mother had made the agreement to have me at the barn. When I got there, the farm owner expected me to know what was going on. It seemed that I was always "behind the eight-ball" so to speak. With my mother's drinking, I was continually broad-sided by other people's expectations. I was in the dark and often in a state of anxiety about the unexpected. At times, people seemed upset with me for reasons I couldn't figure out. One of the conclusions I drew about myself was that I wasn't able to understand people or the world. It was all too confusing, and somehow I lacked something that others had that made it easier for them.

Specific to the barn event, I concluded that I was replaceable – any little girl could replace me. My mom cared enough to get me a horse, yet cared so little about me she forgot the appointment at the farm. I decided that maybe she didn't really care about me; or that she had, and that I'd done something wrong and now she didn't. It was often like this with my mom.

I had absorbed the idea that I wasn't worthy enough to be included and would somehow keep missing out. Furthermore, out of the farm owner's anger, I perceived I had done something wrong – though I didn't know what – and that I deserved her anger.

My mother often forgot things. Sometimes she'd even forget and leave me somewhere. Part of my response to this was to assume that there was something wrong with me. I didn't sit down and say to myself, "She left me, therefore I must be flawed." It was more a process of seeing how life worked. Things went out with the trash. Things that weren't wanted were left behind, so I must fit that category. I had accepted and applied meaning without even questioning it.

I also felt that I wasn't deserving, that I wasn't good enough. Even when good things came into my life, I was uncomfortable and at the same time felt guilty for having them.

When I first found out about deserving, I had a child's view on it. I saw deserving as more materialistic: I deserve this thing, I deserve that success.

It took some diligent work to get to the place of understanding that deserving functioned on a deeper level. As I kept up with my processing, I found more internal freedom and began to allow deserving on a deeper level. Working from the outside in – going deeper and deeper – I noticed my levels of deserving also went deeper, too. It wasn't just about deserving things and successes. It addressed some of the shame, too. I began to feel I deserved to be here, to have my life, and to have impact on others.

Some people see deserving as entitlement, but there is a difference. Deserving has humility within it. Deserving unfolds. Entitlement is a kind of demanding. Some people go around saying, "I deserve this, and I deserve that," with an angry urgency. It is almost an energy of, "That should be mine. Give it to me." This isn't deserving as I understand it.

Out of these decisions – that I wasn't good enough, that I was easily replaced, that I was flawed, that I would be forgotten, and that I didn't deserve – I felt I needed to make myself indispensable. In situations and groups, I became a workaholic. I didn't want to be replaced again. I used this to soothe my low self-esteem and feelings of unworthiness.

Another arena affected by "what it means about me," was my ability to trust. I determined at an early age to do as much as possible – if not everything – by myself. My mother wasn't trustworthy and I didn't know how to truly trust myself. Learning to ask for and receive help was another growth curve for me. Sometimes I had my back to the wall and I could do nothing but allow the help in.

Every time you ask for help and are able to receive it, a little more of the "I can do it myself" attitude dissolves. When you allow yourself to be vulnerable and receive support, you find that you aren't alone. It takes courage to receive.

I found it challenging in that to receive, I had to trust. Trust wasn't something with which I had a good relationship from my early experiences. I had patterns that drew untrustworthy people to me. Gradually, I worked with releasing those patterns so I could allow people who were trustworthy into my life. It's not perfect, but I'm a lot clearer about it. I've learned to trust myself more in being able to discern who and who not to trust.

What That Means About the Other Person

Another layer, or level, is that we decide what this means about other people. Sometimes it is that other people can't be trusted, are mean or only want to use me that create the conclusion that there is no good in the world. As those decisions get cemented, they become filters through which we view reality. We begin living through those filters, and that's what we attract to us.

We can also come to the conclusion that others are better than us. To offset that, some people tell themselves, "I'm spiritual, I'm a nice person." In some way, they're trying to feel better in their own eyes.

The most constant person I had to make decisions about in my life was my mother. Her mixed messages led me to decide that people don't really love you when they say they do, can't be relied on, and for the most part, cannot be trusted. Some of my mother's friends used her. I saw that and decided people only want to use you for their own ends. I began to live from a very guarded place, not knowing who I could trust or when.

One of the decisions I made about others was that people couldn't be trusted; they would let you down. There are times when, of course, people do let you down. But out of this early decision, I approached everyone with the expectation they were going to let me down.

In an interesting kind of twist, I began trusting the very sort of people who were most untrustworthy. As children, we are taught that we should trust our parents, teachers, clergy and other authorities. I had conflicting messages: trust/don't trust. Out of this I began to trust what was most familiar, what I had seen as a child. The pattern was set to trust those who would take the most advantage of me.

I assumed everyone was like this for many years and attracted many people who would take advantage of me. As I began to heal, that pattern shifted and I allowed in more and more trustworthy people. I had to change those decisions and beliefs, and even then I'd slip back into the pattern at times. I developed a little self-alarm that if I instantly felt trust for someone, I needed to take a second, closer look and let some time go by to see if that trust was warranted.

I'm sure there were perfectly great and trustworthy people I met, but because their energy of trustworthiness wasn't familiar for me, I shied away from them. It was frustrating for them. Later in my process, some of them shared with me how it felt like they were on trial around me. They could sense an expectation and didn't know what it was, or felt they were falling short. No one could be perfectly trustworthy for me and they could feel that. Having done a lot of clearing and healing, this has changed. My friendships are much more mutual and there is room for mistakes on both sides. Deeper freedom requires a need to recognize these patterns, and work with and release them.

Another assumption I had made was that people are hard – if not impossible – to understand. I seemed to always make mistakes in communication and was baffled by their responses. My mentor, the horse trainer, helped me with this. He saw how I was struggling. Later, he would talk to me about what people expected and how I was making them mad. He helped me begin to see and understand people and why they reacted the way they did. His influence was immeasurable, but I am only touching on it here as it would require another book in itself.

Even with my mentor's help, many of the deeper pains were still active in my life. The more I lived my life from these points of view, the more I encountered situations that validated them. Over and over, my limiting beliefs were strengthened. That became my reality until I began my inner work. I discovered I needed to look at these layers and levels, and clear them along with the original hurt and pain.

There is a lot of dialog today about "oneness." We are all one and there really is no separation, and at the same time, we live in a dual reality. If you have beliefs that people are always better than you or that you're superior to them, or they're out to get you, what kind of oneness will you experience? It's important to realize that these filters are what need to change. As you change the filters, then what you bring to you is healthier for you.

What that Means About the World

"The world was a confusing place and I didn't fit in with it." That was the biggest assumption I made about the world. I also felt that the world didn't want me. By the time I was in my teenage years, I had the idea that somehow I had been sucked up in a giant vacuum and dumped in the world by mistake. I felt out of place and couldn't figure out how to belong. Things were so confusing for me, and whenever I looked at other people functioning with apparent ease, I felt I was in the wrong place. And my mother, with her drinking, wasn't there to help me sort through things.

I had some pretty heavy-duty filters in place; I wasn't wanted, wasn't good enough, able to be replaced, no one was trustworthy; people were irrational and angry for seemingly no reason. Just the conclusions I'd drawn about myself and others made for an unhappy experience in the world.

The world became a place of struggle for me, something to fight against and overcome. Not overcome in the sense of conquering, rather more in the sense of not letting it get to me as much as it did. In my teens, I wanted to follow my dream of working with and training horses, and have the world just leave me alone.

I never considered my relationship to the world at large. I had adopted the position of, "You leave me alone and I'll leave you alone." It was something I was prepared to endure for as long as I was here.

Though my spiritual growth, I began to see the world in a new way. Initially, it was a place to learn lessons. I was surprised when I encountered people who saw the world as a playground to grow, explore and have fun. I tried that on and it didn't work, because I hadn't changed my patterns and beliefs. I kept attracting more of what I'd already had. But as I worked with this facet of my growth, my relationship with the world changed and continues to evolve. I now believe we are here to have a living, interactive and loving relationship with the world.

QUESTION EXERCISE

After you've worked through some of the emotions, look back at what happened and ask yourself, "What did I think this meant about me?" Look also at what you wanted to happen that didn't happen. What did you think that meant about you? These decisions can become beliefs that take root, and then form a filter through which you see and experience life.

In going through the process, begin to look at what decisions you may have made. If you're having trouble seeing some of these thoughts, decisions and beliefs, ask yourself, "What would a person think or believe about themselves if this had happened to them?" See if any of the answers ring true for you.

Below are some questions that may help you discover more. Work with the questions in the same way as you did in the section on questions about your mother found in Chapter 4 - Beginning the Healing.

Think of an incident you have been working with, and when you've got the feelings of it, do this exercise. Pdf version of this exercise can be found at

http://nicolelawrence.com/doors-to-transformation-exercises/

This happened to me because:

1. _____

2. _____

3. _____

4. _____

5. _____

6. _____

7. _____

8. _____

When this happened, I thought I was:

1. _____

2. _____

3. _____

4. _____

5. _____

6. _____

7. _____

8. _____

Because of this, other people think I:

1. _____

2. _____

3. _____

4. _____

5. _____

6. _____

7. _____

8. _____

I don't understand why they did this. I must be:

1. _____

2. _____

3. _____

4. _____

5. _____

6. _____

7. _____

8. _____

I couldn't stop/change this, therefore I:

1. _____

2. _____

3. _____

4. _____

5. _____

6. _____

7. _____

8. _____

Because of this, I'm not allowed:

1. _____

2. _____

3. _____

4. _____

5. _____

6. _____

7. _____

8. _____

When I think of this incident, I think other people are:

1. _____

2. _____

3. _____

4. _____

5. _____

6. _____

7. _____

8. _____

Because of this, life is:

1. _____

2. _____

3. _____

4. _____

5. _____

6. _____

7. _____

8. _____

Because of this, I can:

1. _____

2. _____

3. _____

4. _____

5. _____

6. _____

7. _____

8. _____

Because of this, I can't:

1. _____

2. _____

3. _____

4. _____

5. _____

6. _____

7. _____

8. _____

In review, there are more layers and levels to explore in the healing process. I realized I needed to clear these additional layers of meaning if I was to come to peace with my mother. The abuse (or in my case neglect) happened and has its own emotional field that needs to be released and healed.

Beyond the levels and layers, we need to look at What Didn't Happen That I Wanted to Happen, What That Means About Me, What That Means About the Other Person, What that Means About the World, to discover what decisions and beliefs are still operating.

In this chapter, I've mentioned feelings of shame. Shame can be insidious. It can color what we see, feel and believe about ourselves at the deepest levels, and I feel it deserves its own chapter, which follows next.

Chapter 6
Encountering Shame

When I revisited the memory of Mom's forgetting the photo of me with my horse, I felt the feelings of hurt and pain. Along with these were feelings of shame – shame that I'd missed out and feeling ashamed that my mother wasn't more responsible. I had a lot of anger at my mom for her drinking, in her forgetting. There was also the devastating feeling that I could be so easily replaced. That feeling of being replaced was also a feeling of shame.

Most people with difficult childhoods end up having to deal with shame. There is a kind of shame for the behavior that we did, that we feel remorse for. Another kind of shame, one most often experienced by those in dysfunctional families, is the shame of being. Lazaris explains these really well in his series of recordings on shame at different ages in our lives. Another good source for healing shame is John Bradshaw, author of "Healing the Shame that Binds You."

The shame of being comes about from abuse where the child feels not that they have done something wrong, but that who they are is wrong. Society holds that parents know best, and when abuse happens, the child feels they are at fault.

I was really startled by what I discovered when I began exploring my shame issues. I had harbored a life-long feeling that there was something wrong with me, but I could never pinpoint what it was. Shame from early life can be so pervasive as to become an accepted way of life. One of the ways my shame showed up was any time someone near me was angry, I would feel guilty and apologize – even if I wasn't the focus of their anger. At a deep level, I felt I had to apologize just for being alive.

With the shame of being, there is the feeling that you are a mistake. Feeling shame leads to remorse for something you've done. You can ask for forgiveness, and seek to change and be different. With the shame of being, there is the sense that you are the "wrongness," and you feel you cannot change or be fixed.

It has an impact at the core level of your being that affects self-worth, self-esteem, self-confidence and your ability to give and receive love. It generates a negative self-image, out of which can come lowered expectations of yourself and the world.

Until I began to work with and understand my shame, I unconsciously spent a lot of time and energy trying to be helpful as a way to make up for it. When I first began the journey of self-improvement, I was looking for the elusive "thing" that I could feel was wrong, but couldn't define. I thought that if I could just find it, I could fix it.

From living in a state of shame, beliefs and patterns form. Along with releasing the painful memories of the events, the patterns and beliefs that hold them in place need to be released and changed as well.

Some of the shame beliefs I discovered and worked with were:

• I don't have a right to be here.

• Nobody loves me – nobody can love me.

• Love doesn't want me.

• I am a failure.

• I don't have a right to_____.

(I could fill in the blank with practically anything on the last one.)

Getting stuck in living from apology is one facet. Another facet I found was looking for permission outside of me. I needed the shoring up of authority figures for permission in many areas of my life; for instance, to take on a project, for confirmation that I did a good job, that my opinions were correct. Most people seek guidance and support in their life, and this is normal. What I experienced was a paralyzing self-doubt. As long as I had approval of those around me, I could keep going. Without that, I tended to grind to a halt.

Sometimes people have doubts about their vision and creative process, and even with those doubts are able to follow through to completion. This can be a normal part of the creative process, to pause, question and refine. But with the shame of being, it can be difficult for a person to become self-actualized. The natural process of stopping to question becomes an inability to move forward because of a lack of adequate approval, not refining of vision.

As I healed my shame, I came to trust myself more and was better able to sort out the natural process of refinement from approval seeking. I was also more willing to take risks and see whether they turned out to be mistakes or successes.

When unhealed shame is operating, it also makes it difficult to hear constructive criticism – it lands on the sore spot of the wrongness of the shame. With the shame of being, it can be hard to separate out your work from your identity. Criticism, even constructive criticism, can feel like an attack on who you are.

I've found the shame to be in layers, like much of the emotional work I've done. I work and make progress, and then more realizations and understandings come up. It is a process. When I first learned of shame, I focused exclusively on it with the idea I could eradicate it all at once. I've since found it is a process. Deeper layers reveal themselves as I'm ready to handle them.

Lazaris says that one of the things about shame is you cannot totally clear it by yourself. Because of the nature of shame, you need to ask that it be lifted by a connection you consider a Higher Power – God, Angels or Higher Self – allowing something more than you, the Divine, to intervene. He goes into the process for doing this in the recordings.

Our beliefs and patterns operate from our subconscious mind like computer programs. So even with releasing emotions and healing shame, we need to address these "inner programs." In the next chapters, I will take a look at beliefs and patterns, and the effects they can have.

Chapter 7
Beliefs and Patterns

The various meanings and conclusions we come to add layers to the original event that happened. We are often not aware of making these decisions and choices. They are the secret, invisible lies that we live with, assuming they are truth. We tell ourselves explanations about why they are true. New decisions and meanings are layered on top of other decisions and meanings that we already believe about ourselves.

An example of this is a spiritual group I was involved with in the early 1980s. There was a great gal I knew there, Ann, and she was able to get people to hear her when she said 'no.' Chronic to this organization, as in many New Age groups where volunteers are relied upon, there were not enough people to do what needed to be done. Those of us most closely involved took on the lion's share of the work, often overdoing and burning ourselves out.

We were both on "staff," and the people at the top kept putting things on us, more and more projects and tasks to accomplish. It always amazed me that Ann could go and tell them that she couldn't do any more and they'd listen to her. I asked her how she did it. She said she just went to the meeting and told them sorry, she had too much to do already and couldn't take any more on.

I tried that. It didn't work for me. I'd meet with the head or one of the managers and tell them I had too much to do and leave having agreed to take on even more. I couldn't figure out how she did it. I tried techniques from assertiveness trainings I attended and techniques from books I'd read, but nothing seemed to work. I was frustrated. Ann, they could hear. Me, no.

I've since learned this is because we had different beliefs about people being there for us, people hearing us. Out of this basic belief that people couldn't be there for me and hear me, I was attracting a reality to match that.

Repeat behaviors are often referred to as patterns. Some patterns are blaring and easy to see, while others can be difficult to uncover. We are so used to living with them they become "normal." We take for granted that this is what life is like. That sense of familiarity keeps the pattern going. We become a magnet for people who fit the other pieces of that pattern, often finding ourselves in relationships and friendships, attracting the same types of people and events over and over again.

It's as if you have one half of a zipper, and people or circumstances have the other half. The half of the zipper I had was reliability and the willingness to do it for approval. The other half of the zipper was people who wanted someone else to be the workhorse.

It's important in looking at these patterns that it's not just a mental exercise. As with emotions, when you do the work of feeling and releasing, clarity comes. When you release and express emotions, insights can surface more readily. It is not something you can think your way to.

Looking at my life, I could see things weren't working for me. For instance, people wanting so much from me; wanting me to be the one to make things happen, to get the job done and do the lion's share of the work. It was a mystery to me why this kept happening.

As I went through my process, I could see that this stemmed, in part, from my mother's reliance on me and the approval I got from her for that. Early on, I accepted the identity that I was the one who people could rely upon. While being reliable is important, it doesn't serve you or the other person when it supports dysfunctional behavior.

Patterns often reveal themselves as you do your process. I became aware that I was a magnet for the other half of the pattern, and that my life wasn't going to change unless I changed the patterns in me.

As well as seeing patterns as they arise during your process, it can be helpful to do a little detective work, too. Discovery can come from the questions you ask about meaning - in Chapter 5 - The Layers of Process, we asked the questions:

What does this mean about me?

What does this mean about others?

What does this mean about the world?

You can begin to uncover beliefs and patterns by looking at the answers you wrote down.

For me, I discovered a pattern that I had to do things on my own. This self-reliance worked for me most of the time until I was really sick or injured, or was in need in some other way that I couldn't solve by myself. In the early years, it wasn't so much that I *couldn't* let the help in, as that I *wouldn't* let the help in. I had a strong identity about being able to do things myself. If I couldn't do things for myself, I felt weak, vulnerable and not safe.

I wanted to change that. I had gone from not wanting the help of others to desiring help, but I wasn't able to receive that help. More unraveling had to occur, more healing, more letting go.

These are patterns and beliefs that occur at the deep subconscious and unconscious levels. I had decided to allow in help, but my subconscious mind was still operating under the old pattern of me doing it alone.

There is a lot of good information, books and techniques that teach you how to go in and make changes at the subconscious level to change beliefs and patterns. There are recordings in the Lazaris material on this. I've also used Dr. Medearis's method, Ultimate EFT, to change patterns and beliefs at the subconscious level.

Dr. Medearis works with changing deeply held beliefs and patterns that arise out of trauma. She combined Emotional Freedom Technique (EFT) meridian energy tapping and her methodology, Ultimate EFT, which activates the body's innate intelligence, for a more easy and direct way of changing the subconscious mind. You can find links to the Lazaris material and Dr. Medearis' website in the Resources section.

In uncovering my patterns and limiting beliefs, I was able to see that my mother had her own patterns and beliefs, as well. I know my mother had her sorrows, her hurts and her dashed hopes that she lived with. She was of a generation that wasn't inclined to do this inner work. Without any kind of help, the only way she knew to get away from the pain and confusion was by drinking.

It's helpful to know that these patterns are at work in our lives. They can cripple us if we don't recognize them and do the work to release and shift them to create new patterns.

We find ways to make ourselves feel better about all the patterns and feelings in us that we live with all the time. Beyond the ideas that I didn't deserve help and had to make myself indispensable, I told myself, "It's because I'm special or I'm strong, I can do the work. That's why they want me to do it." I tried to convince myself I was strong and could rise to the occasion. That was on the surface – beneath, there was a feeling of desperately wanting to belong.

It's important to write these down as you see them, as they surface. They are not truth, either. The comparisons and competitions, the "winning" we get into, might feel better for a little while, but in the long run they don't work. The good feeling lasts for a time and the sensation passes away. Then you've got to find another person to be better than or situation to win in order to feel good about yourself again.

If you're like me, you prove yourself by how much you are willing to let people put on you in terms of work, money issues and personal problems, and all kinds of other things. I burned out and eventually saw that I could not live up to this self-created ideal of who I thought I was.

It's important to recognize and realize that none of these explanations are the truth. The truth is you had painful experiences in childhood, and out of that spun a lot of beliefs, attitudes, decisions and choices that you were living under today.

Dominant Vibration

The law of attraction states that what you focus your energy, your mind and intention on is what you will attract. This can work well unless you have patterns that are opposite to what you want. A good source for learning more about this is the Abraham Hicks material.

They also talk about "Dominant Vibration." The dominant vibration is that vibration or resonance which is the strongest in your field of energy. It is the main vibration that you hold. For instance, some people seem to be happy most of the time no matter what is happening in their lives. Others are sad or angry. They find something to be upset about even when things are going well. It is like being in a crowded place with a friend trying to carry on a conversation, then a band begins to play that is louder than the rest of the noise and the music becomes the dominant vibration in the room.

Various parts of you are vibrating, but there are some that will be louder than others. If the loudest ones are constricting patterns that come out of your childhood pain, then they are what are going to show up in your life. Looking at what has been or tends to be your dominant vibration can also help you discover patterns and beliefs.

Consistent patterns color and lend themselves to your dominant vibration. In my case, I expected people to not be there for me, and my dominant vibration contributed to my life playing out that way.

Not all conditioning and patterns happen in childhood years. For some, traumas can come even earlier – in infancy and even in the womb. The next chapter takes a look at these levels.

Chapter 8
Preverbal and Prenatal

We've looked at traumas, beliefs and patterns that happened in childhood. But what about traumas that happened when we were an infant, or even before birth? Sometimes our mothers go through something when they are pregnant with us and this can have an effect, too. I encountered this in a pattern that had been there all my life.

There is a whole field of study and healing dedicated to preverbal and prenatal conditioning. Rebirthing is one, and Arthur Janov's work, Primal Therapy, is another to mention.

Every time I was planning to go somewhere – a workshop retreat or some other type of event – my mind would come up with reasons why it wasn't going to happen. Images and thoughts surfaced of me arriving and being told that I couldn't be there, that there had been a mistake or that I didn't belong. No matter whether it was putting my artwork in a show or going on vacation, there was always this underlying mental scenario that I would be rejected at the last minute.

I'd put my attention and focus on other things, and the moment I let my guard down, the imagery would be back. With the images, I kept cycling through worry and fearing rejection. Out of this fear and the expectation, I often "ejected" myself (rejecting myself) out of the situation before rejection could happen. The pattern my mind was feeding me felt so real that it stirred up a lot of emotions.

From processing and exploring this pattern, I discovered some of its roots. When I was around five years old, I remember my mother telling me that she hadn't wanted to be pregnant with me. She said she'd gone to two different doctors and begged to get an abortion, but they wouldn't help her out – 1957 was a different era. Pregnant is not what my mother wanted to be. From what I've heard, my parents' marriage was already in trouble. To give her credit, Mom always followed up the story of not wanting me by saying she was glad she did have me.

Even though Mom told me she was glad she had me, those initial messages of rejection stuck in my little mind. Also, at the time she wanted an abortion, that message of rejection was received by the fetus.

I understand now that at the cellular level, the rejection feelings remained. It most often showed up as feelings of not having the right to be here. It took me a long time to realize that my trying to make myself small, to in a sense disappear, was in part coming from this. The images anticipating rejection were mind loops, and out of this I'd reject myself. I also realized it was a source of deep shame, what Lazaris refers to as the shame of being.

As I became aware of the pattern, I was curious about what lay behind it. Early on, I'd just react to the pattern. I'd tell myself it would all be fine and there was nothing to worry about. But even with all of that self-talk, I was still miserable because I kept having these feelings and my mind kept up its negative imaging. I found I was trying to process feelings that weren't based on any fact of reality, but on imaginings. It was really frustrating.

I dove into this pattern because I was seeking peace and release from constantly expecting rejection. I felt the feelings and looked inside to see where it was coming from – whether it was my inner child or my inner adolescent or some other part that was fearful and expecting this outcome.

In working with this pattern, I discovered a kind of compensation for the pain. I noticed a second, more subtle feeling beneath the rejection. It was a feeling of "rightness" to the pain I was feeling. It came and went very quickly.

At first, I judged it and pushed it away – "It couldn't be right to be rejected." But I was curious, so I dove into those feelings and followed a thin thread of the 'rightness of the pain.' It was similar to when you have a sore muscle and you rub it, how it will sometimes feel good. I leaned into that 'right' feeling. I began to explore and ask why it seemed right.

Insights began to surface. I saw I was creating pain for myself so that there was something I could control. In a sense, the pain I could control was easier to deal with than the pain I couldn't control. Creating pain for myself with my mind had become a habit over the years.

It isn't that I wanted the rejection or that I liked the pain. It's no fun when your mind runs loops of negative scenarios. Habits in our mind become ingrained and can be stubborn to get unstuck. Sometimes it still shows up, but I know what it is now. I can allow the feelings and forgive myself.

It takes attentiveness and diligence to work with this kind of pattern. When I catch myself running one of these scenarios, I apply one of the techniques I've learned.

Particularly helpful for pre-birth and preverbal trauma for me has been the Trauma Clearing Technique developed by Dr. Medearis for working with the subconscious mind. The subconscious mind holds all of our beliefs and patterns, and plays them out in our lives. This is where the mind stores prenatal and preverbal conditioning. The subconscious mind needs to be involved to change these beliefs and patterns.

Working with patterns and beliefs is only one part of what goes into healing the past. We have within us different parts that make up the whole of who we are. It can be beneficial to check in and work with these parts, as well.

* * *

Chapter 9
Our Inner Child

In addition to creating conscious memories, our childhood experiences live on in what is known as the Inner Child. That child is a very real presence within us. Our Inner Adolescent and Inner Young Adult each have their own memories, too. An entire book could be written on the various parts, but for this book I'm focusing on the Inner Child.

Lazaris took us through many meditations to meet and work with our Inner Child. When I first heard about the Inner Child, I didn't give it much credence. I thought it was just another tool to access the painful hidden places. I was really surprised at what transpired.

On a visualization exercise, we went to a safe place in nature. There, we invited our Inner Child to come to us. That young me was dressed as I would have been, even down to the little red Keds™ sneakers. What surprised me was that my Inner Child began to do and say things that weren't part of the meditation. It was totally spontaneous and very much who I was, even at that young age.

Exercise to Meet Your Inner Child

Choose a 10- or 15-minute time period where you won't be disturbed. Sit or lie down in a comfortable position, but one where you won't fall asleep. Now take a few deep breaths and close your eyes.

Begin to think of a beautiful place in nature. It can be a place you've been or some place in your imagination. Notice the colors, the smells and sounds. Reach out and touch something – a flower, tree, the grass on the ground, and notice how it feels.

Now, think of yourself as a child, as you were around the age of five or six. It is OK if you don't have a strong image; just get a sense of that child you. In your place in nature, see that child you playing. They haven't seen you, the adult you, yet; so just watch them.

After a time, they notice you there and they approach. They'll ask you who you are. Tell them, "I am your future self, who you will grow up to be." They don't find this odd or strange and they believe you. You can tell them, "I'm here to talk with you, to help you, to listen to you."

Let them take you by the hand and show you some of the fun things they've found in this beautiful spot in nature. They may even tell you stories about what they discovered. Just be with them.

After a time, ask them, "Can I give you a hug?" They say, "Yes." Enfold them in a hug and just hold them. Feel their small body and their hands on your back.

When you are done with the hug, let them know you'll be back to visit them again and they can find you in this beautiful spot in nature.

Wave goodbye and come out of meditation. Open your eyes when you are ready.

* * *

Sometimes, in doing inner work, we can call upon one of those parts, such as the Inner Child, to help us get a deeper perspective on an issue we are healing. Many of my insights about how I felt and what I thought that meant about me I got from working with my Inner child. Beyond just getting insights, we also worked directly with healing our inner child, and this also has had a profound impact on my health and happiness.

Another way to work with the Inner Child is to ask the discovery questions from Chapter 5, but ask from the Inner Child's perspective.

Decide beforehand what you want to work on, but be open for it to change as the most appropriate memory will come up. You can do this by going into a meditation or inner visualization. Talk to your Inner Child. Tell them you want to heal this event that happened. Ask them, "When it happened, what did you think that meant about you?" You can also enter into that small body and ask yourself, "What did I decide this means about me?" Continue in whatever way you are working to ask the other questions; "What does this mean about them (the other person)?" "What does this mean about the world?"

You may be surprised at the answers you get. Thank your Inner Child and give them a hug. They may want you to sit and listen if they have more to say about what happened. Just be with them.

When you are ready, come out of meditation and journal what you received.

* * *

There are many techniques, good books and counselors who have written about and done work on the Inner Child. One among many, John Bradshaw, did a lot of writing and work with the Inner Child and also shame. By working with and building a rapport with the inner child, you can get more immediate insights into the issue you are healing. Be sure to take time to develop a relationship with your Inner Child. They are not just a tool for processing, but are a living part of you. Treat them tenderly and with respect.

With all this work on ourselves, it can be helpful to look at how we've divided up our life's experiences – our defining moments. Sometimes making a subtle shift in this area can make all the difference.

Chapter 10
Changing the Milestones

There's something I call the milestone phenomena. Other teachers and writers talk about a milestone as a defining moment or event, good or bad, that had an impact on us and could be life changing. When one of these events occurs, there is a tendency to see life as "before" and "after" that milestone.

When I was in my 40s, I lost a number of people in a short period of time. These individuals were from different parts of my life; some were family, others were friends. It took me two years to go through the grieving process. I did go to a counselor for help with that; it was too much for me to deal with on my own.

I needed the support and encouragement because these losses put me in a very difficult place. Death has a tendency to make us look at what is important and review our values. Having many people die in a short period of time brought me to a huge life review.

Many things that had been important to me previously were no longer important. My relationship to holidays and birthdays changed, as the majority of the people who passed away were the ones connected with these celebrations. Whenever I went out, I saw places – stores, restaurants, gathering places – that reminded me of those who had passed away. It was a challenging time for me.

I was working with the Abraham-Hicks material toward the end of that two-year healing period. I learned from their teachings that we define ourselves in different ways. I realized I could define myself as the person to whom all this loss happened. I could see my life as who I was before and after those deaths. If I did that, the losses became the milestone, and I'd be identifying myself as the one to whom it happened.

It did happen to me, but instead, I chose to make the milestone something different. I moved the focal point from the deaths, "This terrible thing happened to me," to "I healed from this and am stronger for it." This doesn't mean I went into denial or avoided my process of grieving. I still went through the feelings. All the losses very close together did have an impact and I did change from it.

The milestone I chose was not the sorrow and loss, but the strength and the healing. When you focus on the trauma as a milestone, you can see yourself as the victim of the events and begin to define yourself by that.

I'm not advocating ignoring your emotions, especially if you were a victim. Definitely feel and process those emotions to release them. It is natural to focus on the events themselves at first. Further into the healing, there comes a point where you decide how the event is going to fit into your life. Am I going to live as the victim of this or as the survivor? It is vital to do the emotional work before taking this step. Jumping into shifting the milestone focus can result in unclear emotions. For me, shifting my milestone focus came in the latter part of the two-year healing period.

In reviewing your childhood, see if there are any painful events that you are holding as a milestone. Look to see how you are defining yourself because of it and see if there is another choice you could make. One possibility is to be the one who healed from that trauma, or the one who overcame and integrated the positive of that experience into their life.

All of this inner work leads to freedom and forgiveness of ourselves and others. A big part of forgiveness for me lay in understanding. The more I could understand my mother, the more I was able to forgive her.

Chapter 11
The Seeds of Understanding

What we don't understand, and is important to recognize, is that our parents were once children with their own aspirations, hopes and dreams. They had ideas of what they wanted to be when they grew up and the kind of life they were going to lead. They had friends. They kept the secrets of childhood, and made up secret names and meanings only their playmates understood. They had moments of irritation with their parents; groaned and complained to their friends about how out-of-touch their parents were. Along with their high hopes and dreams, they suffered losses just like we did. Their lives didn't turn out the way they'd imagined as children.

* * * *

Every winter before we were split up, Mom took the three of us kids ice skating. There was a public indoor rink near where we lived. My elder siblings, Debbie and Larry, seemed to eagerly jump out onto the ice. I started out tentatively, holding onto the wall. Mom, lacing my boots would remind me, "Remember, don't let your ankles fall in, keep them straight."

Clumping over to the ring, I'd begin by pulling myself hand over hand along the wall. People whizzed by, scarves flying as they chatted and moved easily across the cool, glassy surface. My brother zigzagged in and out of skating couples, pretending to be a hockey player.

"Nicole, let go of the wall. You'll never learn to skate that way," Mom called as she circled in her short, fluttering skirt and leotard top.

Eventually I'd let go. Waving my arms for balance, I'd drift into the flow of action hoping no one would knock me down. My skates wobbled over the ruts and divots in the ice, sometimes precariously separating. After a few times skating, I'd get my confidence and venture right out on the main part of the ice, chasing after my brother as he wove in and around tottering people who called out, "Watch it, kid!"

Mom made sure that we each had some skating lessons. I was still a beginner. The hardest part for me was trying to skate backwards, and I never did learn to jump.

My mother loved skating. Stepping onto the ice with one easy push of a blade, she'd glide on one foot to the center of the ring. Seemingly with no effort, she'd be facing the other way skating backwards, picking up speed as her feet wove a crossover rhythm. With a pause and brief look over her shoulder, she'd lift into the air spinning, then float back onto the ice to land on one foot, arms outstretched, her back arched and hair flying.

It was disconcerting to see her skating backwards; especially at those times she'd fly past talking to me as I pulled myself along the safety of the wall. She never seemed to need to look where she was going, and never bumped into anyone. She spun, jumped and floated. We saw her do this and it seemed normal and natural. I assumed all parents were the same; everyone's mom could take off like a gazelle and land like a ballerina.

* * *

As a young teenager I loved exploring, out in the neighborhood and inside; sometimes in my mom's things. My mother had a large wooden trunk she called a hope chest. It was always in her bedroom in whatever house we lived, and seemed to house blankets. I had never paid much attention to it until one afternoon I wanted to see just what all was in there and explore every corner of it.

I lifted the lid and stuck my hand inside. I found musty blankets, pensioned-off sheets and old clothing. More by feel than sight, I stretched deep into the chest, ferreting my way down to the bottom.

Pay dirt! My fingers found a hard edge beneath all the fabric – two boxes about four inches square. Nudging and pulling, I worked them out from under the blankets.

In the light I saw they were old, paperboard jewelry boxes, cracked and yellowed with age. I plopped down on the rug and lifted the lids. Tarnished medals on faded, striped ribbons nestled on discolored cotton batting. I pushed the brittle fabric with my fingers. What were they?

One had writing around the rim and a small imprint of what looked like crossed rifles. Some were round, with small ice skates embossed in the center. Others had writing that was hard to see on the darkened metal.

So intent on the treasure I'd just found, I didn't hear Mom come up the stairs.

"What are you doing?" she demanded.

"Just looking in the hope chest."

"There's nothing in there but a lot of old junk," she sighed. "I wish you wouldn't go poking around in my things."

"Mom, what are these?" Leaning back against the honey-colored wood of the chest, I held out a box to her.

"Those are medals I won," she said, looking in at them.

"But, what are they? How did you win them?"

"They are for swimming, diving, and shooting. I won them years ago."

Looking in the other box she said, "These I won for ice skating."

I saw a flicker dance alive in her green eyes. I kept silent, hoping for more.

"Before I met your father, I competed in figure skating. The coaches said I was good enough to go to the Olympics, and I was getting ready to start training." She paused, "But, then I met your father and got married, and had a family."

I was awed, I wanted to hear more.

"That's all in the past now – a long time ago," she said with lingering sadness in her eyes.

Taking the boxes from me, she said, "Please, I want you to stay out of my things." She went into the bathroom and locked the door. I quietly shut the lid on the hope chest and went to my room.

Wow, Mom won those medals. I didn't even know she'd been in competitions. Why didn't she ever talk about it? This was a whole side of my mother I'd never known about.

My mind went to the times she took us skating when we were little. On the ice, I'd watch her skate perfect figure eights and other forms – school figures she called them – gliding slowly and precisely, one foot held in the air. Mom explained how each line in the ice incised by the skate, had to be exactly in the groove made by the blade on the circuit before. It never dawned on me to ask why it was important, or how she knew this. Now, I was thirsty for every detail.

At different times over the years, I tried to locate the medals again, but was unsuccessful. I tried, but was never able to get her to talk about it again. If I asked, she'd simply reply, "Oh, it all happened so long ago, I just want to forget about it."

I never forgot, and think perhaps that is why she gave me so much freedom to explore what I wanted to do with my life. I was never pressed to be or do anything other than what I creatively came up with in my own mind. She totally supported my dream of one day growing up to train horses, or the next to be an artist or whatever it was I imagined myself to be that week.

I discovered that gaining some understanding of why my mother did what she did, why she was the way she was, was an important part of my healing. Perhaps she had regretted giving up her dream of continuing in figure skating. Because she would never talk about it, I didn't know what she felt about it. Knowing it was important to her, I see that it may have contributed to her drinking. Understanding doesn't negate the neglect and pain I experienced from my mom's drinking, but it did help me move toward forgiveness with her.

* * *

In the beginning of my process, I had a lot of judgments that my mom should have been different and done things differently. There is a tendency to see our parents as always just that: our parents. Then I began to try and see her as not just my mother, but as a person in her own right. The more I came to understand my mom, the more the hard knot of unforgiveness unwound in my heart.

When I gained understanding of who she was, her struggles and pain, I had more compassion for her and my judgments began to leave. If I had stayed in judgment of her, I would have had to hold onto the hurts and continue to define myself by them. Those decisions and beliefs had been cemented in place and became the story I carried into the world until I began my healing process. It was the reality that I was living day after day. Then I discovered I could change it. I set to work releasing the emotions, and seeing and changing the beliefs and patterns. As I worked with these, understanding became clearer and clearer.

I found understanding to be a necessary door to forgiveness. In some small or big way, if we can relate to some part of their lives, forgiveness can unfold.

Chapter 12
Forgiveness

Forgiveness is a part of any process of healing abuse. We forgive to release the entangled energies that keep us connected to the other person. We are setting ourselves free as much as them when we forgive. There are many good sources available for working with forgiveness.

In my experience, I have found that forgiveness is more than just saying it mentally. There are times when saying "I forgive you" aloud has impact and creates a softening and release. It's nice when it happens that way. In a case with deeper issues, you may need to address other factors before forgiveness happens. Emotions may need to be released, damaged self-esteem and confidence may need healing, the ability to trust self and others might need work, and coming to a place of understanding the other person all may play a role before forgiveness can occur.

For me, I know I needed to release any unexpressed emotions. As a child, it often wasn't safe to express my feelings. I was told not to talk back and to settle down. I got the impression that I was causing trouble with my emotions. It was years later that I finally expressed many of these suppressed feelings.

Sometimes I felt I needed to be sure of myself - my trust and confidence in myself before I could forgive. The tools of forgiveness I mainly used for my mother were ones Lazaris provided. One thing he encouraged us to be aware of was whether the forgiveness was genuine. If it was, there would be shift within, and I found this to be true for me. There were times I went through the forgiveness process and felt tears, but there was still a knot within me. I knew that a layer may have come off, but I wasn't able to completely let go. Eventually, after more work, it would shift.

I discovered that a large part of getting to forgiveness for me was understanding. As I reviewed my past with my mom and released the old feelings, memories came; like the one of finding her skating medals. With these memories came insights and clarity. I could more easily see my mom's disappointments. I could also see more clearly where I had been holding her to an unrealistic standard. I had wanted a mother who never let life get to her. Mothers weren't supposed to have bad days or dashed dreams. The more I saw, the more human I let her be, and that was a key. Out of that I began to have compassion for her and her journey in life.

That's often the case. It isn't until we are grown that we begin to understand our parents' perspectives. But, we can come to these insights sooner by deciding to work on our past hurts and pains. We can stop blaming our mothers for the hurts and start healing, no matter what. Even if there were a way to get vindication for all that had happened, it wouldn't resolve the patterns and beliefs operating in our subconscious and unconscious minds. We still need to do our own work.

Another thing I learned from Lazaris is that you can forgive someone, but that does not mean you forget. The surest way to not have these patterns repeat is to do the releasing and work on forgiveness. With forgiveness, you set yourself free by forgiving them. Your forgiveness is as much for you as it is for them. Forgiving can release the entangled energies that keep you connected to them and to the patterns.

Sometimes things have happened that we feel are unforgivable. For some, there is no way to forgive the perpetrator. I've found Lazaris's advice in these instances to be helpful. He says, "If you cannot forgive the what, forgive the why." Try to forgive why they did what they did. He explains that forgiving the 'what' will follow over time. Forgiving the 'why' does not excuse or condone their actions. Forgiving the why is part of setting yourself free.

Looking at your life, you may recognize you have brought other people into your life with the same patterns as your dysfunctional parent. You may not consciously want this, yet on some level, because their behavior and energy represents a familiar pattern, there's an instant identification with the person. Not everyone with whom you feel an instant connection represents a pattern from your past, but some people do. Unless you have worked on clearing out these patterns, you can recreate the same relationship over and over without realizing it.

Whenever I've worked with forgiveness, I've always felt lighter and freer, more empowered and in my center. Beyond forgiveness lies the harvest of the gifts revealed through these challenges.

Chapter 13
Gifts From Difficulties

People ask me how I've come to this place of healing. What did I do to be able to come to forgiveness with my mother? I don't see it as any one thing. I explored different modalities, seeking ones that worked for me.

What I've discovered is that the pains and difficulties of my childhood contained strengths that I have learned to integrate into my life. To get to these strengths, I've had to follow my process and do the healing exercises from the various healing techniques. It wasn't always easy and it hasn't been without its challenges. I've had to dig deep within myself, face painful emotions, make changes and learn to be different when I need to be.

The one consistent thing I found to be important was releasing the emotions in some healthy way. This could be writing them out, feeling and expressing them in a meditation or visualization, or using a creative outlet such as painting or even movement such as dance. Suppressing emotions can lead to emotional flare-ups, because we keep them pent-up and the pressure builds. There are some schools of thought that consider suppressed emotions as a possible source for illnesses in the body. Releasing doesn't have to be anything big or explosive; it can simply be sitting with what is being felt and allowing the emotions to flow.

Sometimes people feel just the top layer of emotions and think they're done. Different teachers, coaches and counselors have related that there are layers to emotions, and I have found this to be true for myself. For instance, under the pain I'd find fear, and under that there would be anger. Beneath the anger there might be more fear or hurt, shame or even more anger.

It's important to work down through the layers when they are there. A mistake I made early on in my process was getting off-track and going more sideways than into depth. I'd start with an issue and feel the hurt, and under that was anger. In the midst of feeling and releasing the anger, I'd suddenly remember other events that I was angry about. I'd start following those remembered angers, and soon I'd be off track from the original issue I'd begun with.

Also be aware of staying with the issue or experience related to the emotions. Years ago I was having my car worked on, and when I dropped it off at the garage, the mechanic was very abrupt and angry. I hadn't done or said anything that I knew of – he just seemed angry that I was even there. Nonetheless, it triggered me and I went into some fear and anxiety. I got a ride home, and once there went into the feelings as they were coming up.

The first thing I felt was fear and confusion, and below that, anger. I felt he shouldn't have treated me that way. While I was feeling the anger, I began to think of other people who I felt had also treated me unfairly. Interspersed with these angry thoughts was anticipation about the future - that someone else was going to be angry at me for no apparent reason.

When I was thinking about the past, or assuming and jumping into the future, I was no longer feeling and releasing the fear and anger I had in the "now' with the mechanic. Past events and fears of the future have their place in processing, but I needed to bring myself back to and release the anger I was feeling in the moment. When they surfaced, I made a note of what these memories and anticipations were and returned to the anger I was feeling about the mechanic.

Sometimes these side trips are just that, distractions. Other times, they hold a wealth of information about where emotion has been suppressed. If I were working with a past pain, then that memory and those emotions would be what I focused on. If it triggered something from another time, I'd make a note of that and return to the feelings I'd begun with initially.

It can be easy to get side-tracked, because thoughts and feelings stir up other thoughts and feelings. I had a counselor once who helped me see this. She'd stop me and say, "Just go back to the original issue. Don't worry about that other stuff, we'll handle it later."

Processing the past involves releasing emotions and feelings. Anticipation of the future lies more in beliefs and patterns that we hold. Our subconscious knows the pattern, so the feelings, situations and thoughts that go with that pattern get projected into the future.

Looking back, I can see how the challenges have transformed into gifts that add to who I am. One of these gifts was learning to be more independent. Without my mother to lean on, I had to figure things out for myself. There were a lot of things I learned and taught myself through books, workshops or by talking with friends.

Because my mother was so frequently drunk and unavailable, I had to learn to entertain myself and be all right with being alone. Later, I spent many years in fine art painting in oils, watercolors, pastels and acrylics. As an artist, I needed a lot of alone time. Being alone helped with the ability to spend hours with my creativity, painting or writing.

Another facet of growing up the way I did was that I had to be not just creative, but inventive as well. I had a lot of space to go outside the box; there was no one telling me to stay in. Until I was in school, there wasn't anyone standing over me telling me my art or projects should be a certain way.

An area that was troublesome for me was the ability to say no. Because of my mother's relying on me, I became comfortable with the feeling of over-responsibility. In the jobs that I held, the groups that I joined, I'd be the one staying up late at night doing the extra work. I was the person everyone else counted on to get the job done. It was a familiar pattern – I even felt responsible for things I wasn't even involved in.

Consequently, I overextended myself and have had to heal adrenal fatigue from pushing my body. I've had to learn to say no and stick to it, despite the inner urgings to cave in to demands.

There are many people like me – those who other people want to rely upon. Saying no gives them a chance to rely upon themselves. It can be a gift for them. It can also be a gift to allow others to step in on projects. They find out they are stronger than they knew.

As a child, I set my sights on a very different life from what would be considered normal by society's standards. I wanted a career working with and training horses. While I loved horses, I was also drawn to spirituality and art. My life with horses didn't work out, but one of the positive outcomes of that early focus was that I was willing to embrace something entirely different. At various times I've explored horses, spirituality and art singly and together. I was willing to go off the beaten path to explore the new, so delving into various modalities for healing was natural for me.

* * *

It has been a journey, this life. When I look back to my childhood years, I see how far I've come. I've had to open and go through a lot of new doors. I had to see and come to terms with codependent patterns I learned from my mother. I've had to learn about feeling and releasing emotions, and healing the levels of shame that I was carrying. I've traveled down tributaries of beliefs and patterns, making changes to my inner terrain. I've accepted the need to practice forgiveness and embrace the freedom that comes from it.

It's been a journey of transformation, of learning how to free myself through inner awareness, and applying tools and techniques that have empowered me to grow and change. Working with these may open doors of transformation for you, too.

Chapter 14
Closing the Circle

My mom and stepfather, Michael, were lucky in that they could afford a nurse from a private company to come in at night to help. My mother was no longer able to get out of bed and Michael had begun sleeping in the guest bedroom. He took care of my mom during the day, and having the nurses at night allowed him to get some sleep.

Mom had always liked foot rubs, and after talking with her for a bit, I was happy to give her one. When I pulled back the sheet, I was startled to see her toes and bottoms of her feet had turned a very dark, almost black color.

Somewhere in the past few days, she'd convinced one of the nurses to paint her toenails with coral-colored nail polish. She saw me looking at her feet and said, "Isn't that a lovely color? I like that color of nail polish." As she wiggled her foot, she didn't seem to see the black areas. A few hours later I noticed the blackness was gone and her feet were pink again.

Although I'd spoken with Michael earlier about Hospice, he had until recently resisted calling them because of my mom's reaction to the thought of dying. From all that I'd heard, they were good at helping with people and families in the dying process. In the end, he had called Hospice the day before I arrived. He explained to them about Mom's fears, and she was told they were from another nursing firm.

The Hospice nurse came for about an hour that afternoon, checked Mom and asked if she was comfortable. If she needed an increase in her pain medication, they'd contact the doctor's office and get the prescription changed. Mom was comfortable, she'd been on morphine pills, but hadn't wanted any in the past day.

After the Hospice nurse had seen Mom, I asked her about the blackness. She said that can happen in the last 24 to 48 hours when someone is dying and can also happen in the hands as well. She asked when my sister was arriving. I explained she had four children of her own and wasn't able to get there until the following evening. "I hope your sister is all right with not being here for your mother's passing," she said, adding we were probably in the last 24 hours.

Mom was getting more and more child-like and viewed everything with a sense of wonder, even the Hospice nurses. She said, "Oh, I like these new nurses. They are really good!"

After Mom had a nap, I spent part of the afternoon sitting on the bed with her propped up, leaning on me. She wanted to sit up, but was so weak she slumped sideways with only the pillows behind her. I curled up on the bed beside her and let her lean on me.

She wanted to hear about my trip to France that I'd taken a few weeks before. I'd already made the reservations when I found out she had cancer. At the time, I told Mom that I'd cancel the trip.

"Oh, honey, don't not go because of me," she said. "I've never been to France. Go and come back and tell me all about it."

I'd sent postcards, but she wanted me to tell her in person and in more detail. She'd never gotten to France in her travels and wanted to hear about my trip. I shared about the Louvre Museum and the magnificent art. I got to see Leonardo da Vinci's famous "Mona Lisa."

I shared how I stood in a long line snaking through the hallways of art, waiting to see the famous painting. It was smaller than I'd anticipated, but when I stepped in front of it, there was a magical power about it that was captivating. I told Mom about seeing original Impressionist paintings in the Musèe d'Orsay and how much more alive and colorful they were than in books. I also told about some of the wonderful meals I had there – French cooking is unparalleled.

It was very companionable sitting with Mom leaning on me while I talked. It was an intimacy we'd never before shared. In all my years growing up, her drinking and neediness caused her to figuratively lean on me in inappropriate ways - trying to make me be the parent, to make her feel safe, making me be the one to bail her out of drunken situations.

This kind of physical leaning on me, sitting on the bed with her, felt very right. I held no animosity toward her for any of the past. I was at peace that she had done what she could. Could she have made some different choices? Probably, but she didn't. This is the life I'd had, and if it was different, I wouldn't have had the same lessons and opportunities for growth.

In a way, I was again in the position of being a parent to her, but now it was that of a child assisting a parent who is frail and elderly. There was a dignity sitting with her leaning on me while I brought my trip to France alive for her.

Mom had been agitated when I'd arrived in the morning, but settled down once I spent time with her. Perhaps it was the vestiges of an old "rescuer" pattern from childhood.

It was also surreal sitting on the bed watching Mom's hands and feet turn black for a while, and then go pink again. Sometimes it was her fingers, other times just her palms. She'd talk and gesture with her hands like normal and not notice what was going on, and I didn't say anything, either.

* * *

"Sometimes, in the middle of the night, I think your stepfather is in the room with your mom," the night nurse told me. We were talking, late at night, in the den down the hall from Mom's open bedroom door. This is where the nurses take their night shift with the television on quietly. They can see Mom's bed through the open door and hear if she is awake or needs anything without having to be in the room constantly. "I think I see someone in there and get up to check, but there's no one in the room," she said.

We began to talk about the death process and other spiritual things. I shared that I had heard when someone passes, a relative or loved one who has already crossed over comes to assist them with their transition. I asked her to describe the person she thought she saw.

"He was tall and had dark hair." She knew my stepdad had gray hair, but she kept thinking she saw a younger man in Mom's room with dark hair. She was describing my brother, Larry, who had passed away from cancer eight years before. She didn't know I had a brother. I firmly believe he was coming to help Mom in her time of transition.

In the week before he died, I went to visit Larry. He gave me a very valuable lesson even as the cancer was progressing through his body. I sat with him and sometimes friends would come to visit. One day he told me that it was difficult for him to be around some people. "They mean well," he said, but went on to explain, "When they are talking with me, I can see them begin to think about the past, before I got sick. Or they'll begin to tear up and I can tell they're anticipating the future when I'll be gone. I only have a limited amount of time left. They are in the past or the future and aren't here with me, it's wasting my time." He told me he sent them away, but was nice about it, saying he was tired and needed to sleep. It was such a revelation and spoke of so much truth.

I didn't consciously think it, but I had it somewhere in mind as I sat with Mom, visiting that last day. I listened to where she wanted to go with the conversation and often I just sat in silence with her, sharing the moment.

* * *

Maybe it's just me, but I believe we have help from the Divine when we need it. I also believe in beings such as angels. I had been asking for help for my mother with her passing; to have it be easy and free of fear for her. Asking for help from the Divine – whatever our Source and connection – is something we can do to help a loved one in transition. I wasn't sure what form that help might take, but I trusted it was there and would be there when the time came.

I checked on Mom late at night and her breathing was really labored. With the cancer, her lungs were filling with fluid. I was distressed to hear her struggling to get breath. It was a blessing that she was asleep and didn't wake up. I prayed to the angels, "I know I asked you to help Mom during her time of transition. I'm asking now, can you please help with her breathing? Help her be more comfortable?" No more than 10 seconds after I opened my eyes, her breathing smoothed out; shallower breaths, she wasn't struggling to breathe anymore.

We will all face death one day, in those we love and in ourselves. Modern society in the west has sanitized death to a certain extent that separates us from the immediacy of it. Death makes you look at priorities and your values - it humbles you. If you let it, it can guide you to the seeds of greater gratitude for life and greater compassion for others. It can put you back in touch with the realness of you. Death can open you to tremendous Grace as well.

In the very early hours of the morning, while Mom slept, I sat on the foot of the bed and talked with her. She knew my sister, Deb, wasn't arriving until the evening. "Debbie wanted to be here and is coming as soon as she can, and if you need to go it will be all right," I said quietly.

The nurse came into the room to change my mom's diaper. Tenderly, I helped her roll Mom to the side and then back. My mom had become so thin and emaciated. It really struck me when I saw her body. An insight flashed into my mind: She carried me in that body, she gave birth to me. Mom carried my body inside of hers. She was the doorway for me to come into this life.

The nurse left the room after putting the covers back, telling me she'd be back in a little bit. It was just Mom and me. Her breaths began to grow farther apart. I thought about my stepdad. The day before I'd asked him if he wanted me to wake him if it looked like Mom was passing. "No," he said, "I'd rather remember her as her live, vibrant self."

I sat on the bed next to Mom watching as her breaths slowed, growing farther and farther apart. A gentle peace entered the room. A simple inhale, then exhale and there were no more. After a time, the nurse quietly entered the room. "It's been a while, I haven't heard her take a breath," I told her. Listening with a stethoscope she confirmed that my mother had passed away. One of the things I noticed before the nurse closed my mother's eyes was that they were pale, completely washed of color. The vibrant green was gone.

I sat awhile with Mom before going in to wake my stepdad to let him know. I felt a sense of peace and grace. I was grateful that I was able to be there to offer prayers and hold my mom in love, and that it was a smooth transition.

I realized that being there for my mother, praying for her and asking for help for her crossing, I was in a way holding the door open for her new existence on the other side. She held the door for me to come into this life through her body. I, in turn, held the door for her and thus completed the cycle.

One of my teachers, Lazaris, is fond of saying, "The circle begins where it ends, and ends where it begins." My mother and I participated in a circle of life and death. When parents pass, the daughters and sons become the next generation of mothers and fathers.

Children have participated in the rite of crossing for their parents for eons; from when mankind began. It is a powerful experience of the unbroken chain of humanity. Healing the fear, anger and aguish from childhood not only transforms, but allows the experience of transition and death to be a powerful completion and initiation to a new level.

A Note for Those Adopted

While you may not have come from the body of your adopted parent, they still functioned in symbolic ways of giving birth to you. They were there for many of your firsts: maybe first steps, first time you won an award, or perhaps when you gave birth to your own first child. By opening their hearts and inviting you in, they opened a door for you to enter into a life with them. A door of the heart is not less important, and sometimes more important, than a physical door.

Some online resources and articles for working with adoption issues:

Child Welfare Information Gateway
https://www.childwelfare.gov/adoption/issues.cfm

The Center for Adoption Support and Education, Inc.
http://www.adoptionsupport.org/res/7core.php

Adoptive Families
http://www.adoptivefamilies.com/articles.php?aid=489

Athan, Lisa, MA. Adoption Issues. Grief Speaks website
http://www.griefspeaks.com/id93.html

Patricelli, Kathryn, MA. Long-Term Issues For The Adopted Child.
http://www.amhc.org/11-adoption/article/11455-long-term-issues-for-the-adopted-child

Acknowledgements

First and foremost, I would like to thank Bonnie Groessl and Mike Dauplaise for all of their encouragement, help and especially patience. This book would have only remained an idea without your guidance and support. Much thanks to my mother – I know you did the best you could. It was a perfect upbringing; I got what I needed.

To my sister, Debbie, you filled in the gaps left by Mom and kept me safe. You also showed me the first inklings of what a magical childhood could be. Also to my brother, Larry, for being my sounding board to groundedness. I could have spun off into despair but for your humor and perspective.

Thank you Lazaris, my first steps to true healing came through you. To Liz, for your help and guidance in clearing subconscious beliefs. I'd also like to thank Vima for cheering me on. Being the observer to your discipline and steady progress on your own books inspired me to keep going. To Hileah, you "get" me when others don't and you believe in me. Your words of encouragement have soothed my heart. To Mary Ke, for your insights on the manuscript.

To the Kalaheo Writers Group. Though you disbanded long ago, the months I spent with you helped me find confidence in my writing. To Inette and 'Iokepa, your encouragement and the techniques your suggested for opening to deeper processes with writing were an integral part of this book. Thank you, also, to all the players on the stage of my "Mom lessons." You played your parts to perfection.

Resources

Beattie, Melody. *Codependent No More: How to Stop Controlling Others and Start Caring for Yourself.* New York, NY: Hazelden, Harper & Row © 1992.

Bradshaw, John. *Healing the Shame That Binds You.* Deerfield Beach, FL: HCI Books, © 1988.

Bradshaw, John. *Homecoming: Reclaiming and Championing Your Inner Child.* New York, NY: Bantam Books, © 1992.

Abraham-Hicks. *Ask and It Is Given: Learning to Manifest Your Desires.* Carlsbad, CA: Hay House, Inc., © 2004.

Abraham-Hicks. *Money, and the Law of Attraction: Learning to Attract Wealth, Health, and Happiness.* Carlsbad, CA: Hay House, Inc., © 2008.

Abraham-Hicks Website:
http://www.abraham-hicks.com/lawofattractionsource/index.php

Hay House Website:
http://www.hayhouse.com

Janov, Arthur. *Primal Healing: Access the Incredible Power of Feelings to Improve Your Health.* Pompton Plains, NJ: New Page Books, © 2006
The Janov Primal Center http://www.primaltherapy.com

Lazaris, The Lazaris Material is produced by: Concept: Synergy. PO Box 1789 Sonoma, CA 95476 1-800-678-2356
www.Lazaris.com   ConceptSynergy@Lazaris.com

Medearis, Dr. Liz. "UltimateEFT" & "The Heart's Way." © 2003-2013
http://lizmedearis.com

Murphy, Joseph. *The Power of Your Subconscious Mind.* Paramus, NJ: Reward Books, © 2000

Rebirthing – There are a few different forms of Rebirthing therapy out there and some have come under fire in recent years. The kind I experienced was purely breath work and involved no form of restraint. I was lovingly coached through a breathing process that produced emotional releases. This website describes the breathing Rebirthing process: http://www.mcs.ca/vitalspark/2040_therapies/518rebi.html

Quantum Light Breath – another form of breath work created by Jeru Kabbal. For information, go to: http://www.ahutif.com/quantum-light-breath.php and http://www.jerukabbal.com

Tipping, Colin. Radical Forgiveness: A Revolutionary Five-Stage Process to Heal Relationships, Let Go of Anger and Blame, Find Peace in Any Situation. Louisville, CO: Sounds True, © 2009. http://www.radicalforgiveness.com

Photo by Carrie Mackey Photography

About the Author

Nicole Lawrence is an eclectic soul who has followed her heart to experience careers featuring horses, visionary painting, fine art, event promotion, and exploration of many spiritual modalities. Metaphysics, the New Age, alternative health and healing trends have fascinated her for years.

Never one to follow trends, Nicole's life is a complex mix of ideas and values. Even in her art, she uses a variety of media and subject matter, always seeking and exploring what is over the next hill of creativity. She enjoys the history, stability and familiarity of convention, while at the same time drawn to the "edge of newness," that edge beyond the boundary which gives birth to innovation.

Nicole views life as running in cycles and spirals, comprising the healing journeys we undertake as a regular part of our lives. This book is part of a healing cycle for her. She hopes it inspires others to push through their own journeys of healing.

For more information or to contact Nicole, go to http://nicolelawrence.com.

www.ingramcontent.com/pod-product-compliance
Lightning Source LLC
Chambersburg PA
CBHW071519080526
44588CB00011B/1491